Be Still AND Know

A Month of Meditation

DEANNA ATKINSON

InspiringVoices®

Inspiring Voices books may be ordered through booksellers or by contacting:

Inspiring Voices
1663 Liberty Drive
Bloomington, IN 47403
www.inspiringvoices.com
1 (866) 697-5313

ISBN: 978-1-4624-1305-8 (sc)

Print information available on the last page.

Inspiring Voices rev. date: 08/13/2020

*Thank you, Sam, and daughters,
Amy and Lindsey, for your help,
your enthusiasm, and the
faith that you model every day.*

*Thank you, Sue Edwards, for
reading, fine-tuning, encouraging,
and walking in your faith every day.*

Foreword

I would like to say I often hear God speak to me . . .

I would like to say it, but it wouldn't be true. I have never heard an audible voice from God. I rarely feel a prompting that is so strong that I am certain that it is God. Sometimes I feel a prompting that I think is from God. When God speaks to me, it is most often through the Bible. Imagine that, He speaks to me through His Word!

Two years ago I started writing reflective poetry during a small-group Bible study in my church. When that class was over I wanted to continue writing but didn't know quite where to look for topics. I decided to select Bible verses and reflect on them and write. Actually, I felt that God prompted that idea and that He often led me to certain verses. I found writing helped me meditate on Scripture and brought verses to life. These reflections have enriched my walk with God, and I hope that God will use them to bless your life.

The poems are not arranged in any thematic order: they are simply in the order in which I wrote them.

Day 1

"Be still, and know that I am God; I will be exalted among the nations, I will be exalted in the earth." Psalm 46:10

As a young child I found Psalm 46:10 strange: how could being still help me know anything? What did my level of activity have to do with what I knew? I wasn't too fond of being still. Years passed and I didn't give it much thought. Then the night before my first college test, as I prayed—very nervous about my college performance—this verse came to mind and I understood for the first time. God is God everywhere and in all circumstances. He is my God when life is comfortable and familiar and He is my God when life is hard and scary. I just need to be still and pay attention to Him and His presence. This verse has had a special meaning to me ever since that night when He used it to speak to my heart.

Be Still

Lord, we can hear You best when we're quiet and still,

And it's when we hear You speak that we know what's real:

That You're God of the universe and God of me,

Universal, yet personal—a divine mystery.

The exalted Lord before whom all will bow

Is best known in quiet and stillness somehow.

How like God—He could wield power and might,

But He speaks in whispers; leads us gently into His light.

Quiet my soul, dear Lord. Open my spirit to hear Your whisper. Slow me down and make me aware of Your presence. May every fiber of my soul affirm that You *are* God. Amen.

Day 2

"Rejoice in the Lord always. I will say it again: Rejoice!" Philippians 4:4

"Blessed are those who mourn, for they will be comforted." Matthew 5:4

One morning when I was at the doctor's office for routine blood work, I shared the waiting room with a lady who was obviously distraught as she waited for test results. Her fear and distress were palpable. Throughout the day I thought of her and others who are suffering while the world moves on as usual. Is this what Matthew 5:4 means? Not just mourning when our hearts are aching, but mourning for others who are sad and broken? And realizing that there is always someone who is sad and broken? How can we help bear their burdens? And how does this juxtapose with the admonition to rejoice always?

Rejoicing and Mourning

Lord, You tell us to rejoice but say those who mourn are blessed;

Do You want us to be happy? Do You want us to be distressed?

When things are going well and all seems right in life,

I don't want to think about illness, poverty, and strife.

But then the real world comes crashing in

And I grieve for the suffering, the darkness, the sin.

Rejoicing, mourning—which should it be?

I think it's both simultaneously.

When I see suffering, I'm to empathize and care—

Reach out to the hurting—remember them in prayer.

I can't just ignore them and pretend they don't exist,

I need to do more than add them to my prayer list.

But how can I have joy in the midst of all the pain?

I'll put my trust in You, Lord, and remember that You reign.

So, Lord, I give You my emotions—it's all I know to do;

May I grieve when You grieve and rejoice in what pleases You.

Lord, please reign in my heart. Fill me with love and compassion; make me sensitive to the needs of others and show me how to help. May living in love be the top priority of my life. Amen.

Day 3

"This is the day the Lord has made; let us rejoice and be glad in it." Psalm 118:24

In the '90's we sang this praise chorus so much that I tired of it. The words were more like an old song than Scripture to me. Then on the first anniversary of 9/11, they took on new meaning for me. We were having prayer around the flagpole first thing that morning at school. It was such a heavy occasion and I wondered how our principal would lead our elementary school in prayer. She opened her prayer with this verse. It had such an impact on me and made me love—and really hear—this verse again. Every day is lovingly created by God. We should be grateful for each new day, not dragging in baggage from previous days.

Rejoice in the Day

Triune God, Maker of all my days,

Help me greet You each morning with prayer and with praise.

Remind me that each day is a gift from You;

Help me to rejoice and to be grateful, too.

Open my eyes to the beauty around,

To the love in my life, to blessings that abound.

And even if troubles wait to dampen my day

Show me Your glory, and remind me to say,

"This is the day the Lord has made; let us rejoice and be glad in it!"

Lord, don't let me forget that You made this day and that it is a gift. Open my eyes to Your goodness today—all day—and help me to rejoice in Your blessings and in You! Amen.

Day 4

"In the morning, O Lord, you hear my voice; in the morning I lay my requests before you and wait in expectation." Psalm 5:3

"In peace I will both lie down and sleep, for Thou alone, O Lord, dost make me to dwell in safety." Psalm 4:8 (NAS)

Just two verses I like—plain and simple. I like their simplicity and matter-of-factness. I especially like the expectation mentioned in Psalm 5:3; too often I make my requests but don't really look for and expect answers. It's a good reminder to face the day with prayerful optimism and to look for God's answers and presence.

At night, if I'm alone and afraid, I lie in bed awaiting sleep and imagining "crime show" scenarios. Psalm 4:8 helps—"in peace I will both lie down *and* sleep." I want not only to lie down, but to lie down in peace and also to sleep, trusting God to keep me safe.

Bookends

Perfect bookends for the day—

Morning and evening, remember to pray.

Ask in the morning when His mercies are new,*

Wait in expectation to see what He'll do.

Lie down at night—safe and sure;

Rest in His arms and know you're secure.

Lord, help me to "bookend" my days with prayer. Remind me to begin my day praying expectantly and looking for Your answers. And tonight help me to rest in You, trusting that You're not sleeping, but watching over me and keeping me safe. Amen.

*Lamentations 3:22-23

Day 5

"Jesus Christ is the same yesterday and today and forever." Hebrews 13:8

One night when there had been a lot of bad news on the local TV station, I felt troubled and my soul was heavy. As I prayed that night, wondering what the future held for my young daughters, this verse was impressed on my heart. God used it to encourage me and to remind me that Jesus proved God's power and love when He walked on this earth, and that power and love have not diminished or changed in any way. He is still in charge—always has been, always will be!

The Same

Yesterday, today, and forever the same!

What a testament to Your power and the power of Your name!

Yesterday: Your power is apparent in the past—

Feeding the crowds, healing the sick, redeeming the outcast.

Tomorrow: Sin will be conquered and You will reign;

No more evil, disease, and pain.

Today: Here's where my questions start:

Are my concerns close to Your heart?

Does my little stuff matter? Do You care?

Do You listen to my everyday prayer?

Do You see the evil that's so prevalent now?

Are You still working things together for good somehow?

Plant in me the confidence that You hear when I call,

Whether my needs are weighty or small.

More than answers, may I desire You

And walk in Your will as You'd have me to.

Remind my soul, open my eyes to see

That You're the same as yesterday and always will be.

I praise You, all-powerful Jesus. Help me to live in faith and confidence regardless of my circumstances. You are the same powerful Lord who calmed the storms, fed the hungry, and healed the sick when You walked this earth. Help me to trust You to calm my storms and meet my needs. Amen.

Day 6

"And straightway the father of the child cried out, and said with tears, Lord, I believe; help thou mine unbelief." Mark 9:24 (KJV)

I had Godly parents who brought me up in a Christian home. There has never been a time in my life when I walked away from faith. But I have always had questions and that has bothered me. It seems that one as blessed as I, one who has been nurtured in faith continually, should finally "just believe." No uncertainties, no "am I sure's?"—just solid faith. But that's not always the case. That's why I'm so grateful for this man's faith, but even more for his honesty and his earnest prayer.

Belief

"Lord, I believe; help thou my unbelief."

Thank You, Lord, for the honesty of this man.

I wish I couldn't identify, but I can.

I believe in You, that You came to set all free,

But too often a host of questions washes over me.

11

How could You, Creator God, love all humanity?

More amazingly—how could You love one as fickle as me?

How does Jesus' death atone for every man's fall?

Why do You want a relationship with us at all?

Are You really coming back in power and victory

To take believers home for all eternity?

Thank God my faith is not in my faith, but in You

Because I stand on Your Word and believe that it's true.

Thank You for forgiveness—I don't want to cause You grief.

Lord, I believe; help Thou my unbelief!

Thank You, Lord, that I can bring my questions and doubts to You. Thank You for Your patience with me. I bring my faith to You, with all my questions, too, and ask You to increase it. "Grow me up" in You, Lord. I do believe. Amen.

Day 7

"The Lord is my shepherd; I shall not want." Psalm 23:1 (KJV)

". . . He calls his own sheep by name and leads them out. When he has brought out all his own, he goes on ahead of them, and his sheep follow him because they know his voice." John 10:3-4

"He tends his flock like a shepherd: He gathers the lambs in his arms and carries them close to his heart; he gently leads those that have young." Isaiah 40:11

I understand that sheep aren't very smart animals and that it is not a compliment to be compared to one. Sheep require a lot of care, protection, and guidance. Perhaps that's why Jesus so often refers to us as sheep and to Himself as the good Shepherd. Personally I'm okay with being a sheep as long as Jesus is my Shepherd. I'm grateful for His tender love, His protection, and His provision. And I am grateful that I am in His fold.

Happy to Be a Sheep

If Jesus is my shepherd,

I'm happy to be a sheep.

I rest in soft, green pastures,

I pray Thee, Lord, my soul to keep.

If Jesus is my shepherd,

    He'll show me where to go.

He'll call me out and lead me,

    He knows my name, you know.

He always knows what's best for me

    So obedience is my choice;

When Jesus is my shepherd

    I recognize His voice.

When Jesus is my shepherd

    We're never far apart;

I like it best when He carries me

    Right next to His loving heart.

When Jesus is my shepherd

    He tends me night and day.

I've no desire to leave Him,

    It's in His flock I'll stay!

Yes, Jesus is my Shepherd,

He won't leave me alone,

I'm grateful I belong to Him,

I'm one of His very own.

Good Shepherd, thank You for including me in Your flock. Help me to follow You and not the other sheep. May I rest close to Your heart and in Your care. Amen.

Day 8

"Behold, a virgin shall be with child, and shall bring forth a son, and they shall call his name Emmanuel, which being interpreted is, God with us." Matthew 1:23 (KJV)

I've known for years that Emmanuel means "God with us." So often I think of God's love and the promise of His presence in a collective sense. I know God loves His children; I know God is with His children. Without realizing it, I often fall into the trap of seeing God's love for the whole of creation but overlook His personal, deep love for me. I know God abides with His believers but overlook His promise to be with me, to dwell right inside of me. One Christmas I heard Emmanuel translated "God with *me*" and it took on a whole new depth of meaning for me. Yes, God is with us all—and that includes me. He walks with me and lives in me—one on one. Hallelujah!

Emmanuel

Of all your names, Savior is my favorite one,

Sweet Jesus, my Lord, God the Son.

Because of You I am reconciled:

God is my Father, I am His child!

Emmanuel is another name that I hold dear;

You're not just in heaven—You're also here!

Here within me, here beside me,

Here to love me, here to guide me.

You don't just watch from heaven above

But You're here enveloping me in Your love.

When I feel alone, isolated, it's a lie;

You're in me and close by me—not just somewhere nearby.

Your presence doesn't depend on how I feel;

You're right here with me—Your presence is real.

No matter where I happen to be

You're God with us, God with me.

Emmanuel!

You are my Emmanuel—God with *me*! All the time. Everywhere. Thank You for dwelling in me. Help me to dwell in You. Amen.

Day 9

"You will keep in perfect peace him whose mind is steadfast, because he trusts in you." Isaiah 26:3

Let's face it: we're not always at peace with ourselves and the world. If we're honest, most of us will admit that it's hard not to worry about all the turmoil in our world, in our country, even in ourselves. Honestly, I struggle more with my personal worries than with global concerns. Those I can turn over to God, but I hold my family concerns too close. When my family is in trouble, I worry. I know God will take care of them, but will He do it the way I want Him to? God wants me to give up control, let Him act, and trust Him completely. Then He can give me not just peace, but perfect peace.

Perfect Peace

In His perfect peace is where I want to be—

I in Him and He in me.

What is this—His perfect peace?

It's freedom from fear; it's ease and release.

Not absence of troubles—they're still near,

But the firm confidence that Christ is here,

Living in His peace my fear is replaced:

Instead of fear I choose love and grace.

Who receives peace—this gift so vast?

Those with eyes fixed on Him, whose minds are steadfast.

May my faith be firm, unchanging and true,

Constant and certain as I trust in You.

Can Christ's perfect peace be a reality for me?

According to His Word it's a guarantee

When my mind is steadfast with my trust in Him.

Then He imparts peace—So Be It and Amen!

Teach me, O God, to have a steadfast mind, a mind fixed on You. Keep my mind on Your love and grace and mercy and not on my circumstances. When trouble comes my way, draw my eyes and heart to You. Amen.

Day 10

"For God has not given us a spirit of fear and timidity, but of power, love, and self-discipline." 2 Timothy 1:7 (NLT)

Sometimes fear grips me—fear that something bad will happen to me or to my loved ones. I hate fearing the unknown. I suspect that God hates seeing me succumb to fear, too. Just like I used to reassure my children when they were young that they didn't need to fear things, things that go bump in the night, God must want to reassure me: "You have no need to fear; this fear is not from Me. I give you power and love. Trust Me." That's the bottom line, isn't it: do I trust God to take care of me? Do I believe that He will do what He has promised to do?

No Fear

Father, this fear I feel is not from You.

It comes from the enemy, the father of lies.

What he wants me to believe is not true.

Let me see him as he is—open my spiritual eyes.

Help me to walk in Your Spirit; unleash Your power.

Make fear and timidity foreign to me;

Don't let me fear the future—cringe and cower,

But embrace what's to come: Your perfect victory!

You designed me to live in power and love,

To dwell in Your will with self-control.

You walk beside me, yet watch from above;

Father Almighty—saturate my soul!

Lord, help me to take You at Your word and trust that You are taking care of me. Remind me that I am equipped with power, love, and self-discipline. Father, saturate my soul. Amen.

Day 11

"How great is the love the Father has lavished on us, that we should be called children of God! And that is what we are! . . ." 1 John 3:1

I've been taught all my life that God loves me. I guess I've never doubted it. Yet for years, without realizing it, I have underestimated or left unexplored the depth of His love for me individually. I've never doubted His love for all His creation, for all His children. It's easy to say, "God loves *us*," and "How could He love *us* so much?" But it is amazing and humbling when I begin to comprehend that while His love is for everyone, it is also totally personal—He loves each one. When I think about how much I love my children, I am astounded that God loves me even more since His love is perfect! He loves me enough to adopt me as His child. He is my Daddy! You are His child, a full-fledged member of His family, if you have accepted His invitation.

Family

God is my Father and I am His child, I've known it since I was small;

But I'm not sure I really get it, that I understand it at all.

How can the Creator of the universe—the Creator of me

Want a personal relationship, include me in His family?

He sent His Son to earth His children to redeem

Not to regard as subjects, but to hold in dear esteem.

This blessing isn't delayed to the future—part of a heaven-only plan.

It has already been accomplished; it's who He says I am.

So I'm thankful to my Father that He so loved the world

That He sent His Son to save me and claim His little girl.

Good morning, Father! I'm overjoyed that You see me as Your daughter, a treasured part of Your family. Help me to live up to the family name! Amen.

Day 12

"Come to me, all you who are weary and burdened, and I will give you rest. Take my yoke upon you and learn from me, for I am gentle and humble in heart, and you will find rest for your souls. For my yoke is easy and my burden is light." Matthew 11:28-30

"Come to me, all who are weary and burdened . . ." It sounds so easy—just come. I want to receive God's rest. What holds me back? Perhaps it's time. It takes time to come to Him, to learn from Him. Perhaps it's the yoke. It takes surrender to take on His yoke and burden; yet He promises they are light. Aren't His promises worth it? If I exert the effort to come, if I learn from His gentleness and humility, and if I commit to His way, He promises rest—His rejuvenating rest, rest for my soul.

Rest

Lord, it sounds so simple: "Come unto me,"

But I don't think it's quite as simple as it seems to be.

How do I "come"? How do I pray?

So often I'm preoccupied with the minutia of my day.

In my busy-ness, my schedule, I seek a quick fix;

Distraction is one of the devil's oldest tricks.

Slow me down, Lord; help me take time to rest

In Your loving arms, present with You as Your guest.

I come, Lord.

I come with my burdens of anger and fear;

I approach Your throne, I want to draw near.

I take Your yoke, Lord; I will learn from You.

I want to be gentle and humble in heart, too.

Help me to forgive and let judgment cease.

I guess it's only then that I'll find true peace.

Fear is harder—I have to give up control,

Help me to trust You to guard my soul.

I come, Lord, and take up Your yoke.

You promise Your yoke is easy and Your burden, light;

Lead me into day, out of my soul's night.

May I wear Your gentleness—meek and mild,

Trusting and following as an innocent child.

May I wear humility of soul and heart;

You're the teacher—surrender is my part.

I want to learn from You; please make me whole.

Gentle, humble Jesus, grant rest for my soul.

I come, Lord, and receive Your rest.

Lord, help me to sit awhile with You—to give You my full attention. Show me Who You are—gentle and humble in heart. Help me to take Your yoke; make me willing to be made like You. Wrap Your arms around me and give me Your rest. Amen.

Day 13

"...and we take captive every thought to make it obedient to Christ."
2 Corinthians 10:5

What does it mean to take thoughts captive to make them obedient to Christ? When I think of taking anything into captivity, I think of aggressive, almost warlike behavior. And maybe that applies here. I know my thoughts seem to have a life of their own. I need to be deliberate and determined if I am going to bring them in line with the mind of Jesus. Come to think of it, this does involve warfare—spiritual warfare.

Captive

Lord, the world's vain philosophy

    Is far too often appealing to me.

Living for self seems to make sense

    But somehow it leaves me empty and tense.

Spending and spending and getting more stuff

But somehow it's never quite enough.

Admiring the wealthy, famous, and rich—

But what about me? What is my niche?

EVERY THOUGHT CAPTIVE TO THEE,

OPEN MY EYES TO REALITY.

Others give me a problem, too!

Too often they don't do what I think they should do.

I judge them when I condemn what they've done,

But judgment is Yours and Yours alone.

When I'm wronged, I don't want to forgive and let go

Of the hurt and bitterness that take seed and grow.

Then there's love—the hardest of all,

But to love like Jesus—that's my call.

EVERY THOUGHT CAPTIVE TO THEE,

OPEN MY EYES TO CHARITY.

And then there's You, God—

I hate to say it, but Your ways seem odd.

When my way is hard and I can't understand,

I try to explain You the best way I can.

I put You in a box, wrap it up with a bow,

And try to make You fit with what I think I know.

When I can't explain life, help me to trust

That You're merciful, gracious, all-knowing and just.

EVERY THOUGHT CAPTIVE TO THEE,

OPEN MY EYES TO DIVINE MYSTERY.

Yes, open my eyes, Lord; I don't want to be blind.

Make me like Christ, renew my mind.

Help me see myself as You see me:

Righteous and renewed, complete in Thee.

Help me view others as You view them:

Precious to Christ and redeemed through Him.

And let me glimpse You—mighty and adored,

All-powerful, everlasting, and reigning Lord!

EVERY THOUGHT CAPTIVE TO THEE,

OPEN MY EYES TO ETERNITY!

Lord, remind me that it matters what I believe. It's so easy to slip into the mindset of the world. Lord Jesus, guard my thoughts and let them be pleasing to You. Amen.

Day 14

"Do not be anxious about anything, but in everything, by prayer and petition, with thanksgiving, present your requests to God. And the peace of God, which transcends all understanding, will guard your hearts and your minds in Christ Jesus." Philippians 4:6-7

I hate anxiety—that churning, gnawing feeling in my gut! The fear of what may happen that keeps me awake at night. That's why these verses are among my favorite Scriptures. I committed to pray them for one of my daughters during a stressful time in her life and soon found them extending into my prayers for all my family. Different parts of the verses would stand out at different times—praying with thanksgiving, making specific requests, our hearts and minds being guarded in Christ Jesus. I'm ashamed to say that sometimes I still forget to take my concerns to God immediately. I confess that often I have to pray repeatedly, using this model before I feel God's peace. But I'm grateful for this gracious offer, and I'm grateful that He continues to bring it to mind.

Anxious for Nothing

"Be anxious for nothing"—is that a command?

I'd like to obey, but I'm not sure I can.

Give up my worry, my fret, and my care?

God says to do it with petition and prayer.

Petition and prayer and thanksgiving, too:

Gratitude seems central to all He asks us to do.

I present my requests to Him—perfect release,

And His promised answer is His own peace.

A peace that transcends, we can't understand,

But we can be calm when trouble is at hand.

No promise I'll get what I ask for, in whole or in part,

But better yet, peace of mind and peace of heart.

He sees the big picture and knows what's best,

So He'll do what's perfect with my request.

Then Jesus guards my heart and my mind,

And invites me to leave my anxiety behind.

"Be anxious for nothing"—a daunting call:

It demands my trust and surrender of all.

Help me, Lord, to release all my anxiety to You. Thank You for listening and for working on my behalf. Please guard my heart and my mind with the peace of Christ. Amen.

Day 15

"So we fix our eyes not on what is seen, but on what is unseen. For what is seen is temporary, but what is unseen is eternal." 2 Corinthians 4:18

It's so easy to get caught up in the pettiness of life. I run around trying to accomplish all my personal goals. If I stop and examine my life, some of those things do indeed matter, but much of my busy-ness accomplishes nothing of lasting significance. I want to learn to look at things in the light of eternity and prioritize accordingly. This sounds quite spiritual, but often it's as simple as spending quality time with a child; that's much more important (and enjoyable) than keeping a house in perfect order.

Eternal Significance

Lord, open my eyes to see

Things of importance in eternity.

Help me to see Your reality here

Where truth and significance aren't what they appear.

It's so easy to get caught up in my daily routine

 And obsess over things that are merely mundane.

When I have pressing things to do,

 Remind me to pause and talk with You.

Are they really pressing? Are they key

 To what You have planned and designed for me?

Or are they temporal—time spent in vain?

 Will the fruit they produce bless and remain?

Make me sensitive to what matters to You.

 Awaken my spirit, my senses renew.

Fix my eyes on what's permanent and real—

 Not on my emotions, on how I feel.

Yes, fix my eyes on heaven and You:

 Source of all that's everlasting and true.

I ask, Father, that You'll fix my mind on You and on things that matter. May the things I am busy doing be worth doing. Remind me that I live in Your kingdom now; help me to live like that's true. Amen.

Day 16

"Let us fix our eyes on Jesus, the author and perfecter of our faith . . ."
Hebrews 12:2

Sometimes I put so much pressure on myself. My faith should be stronger. I shouldn't have so many questions. I should just know that I know when it comes to matters of faith. What a relief to realize that it's not up to me to accomplish all these things on my own. I didn't come up with faith on my own: God is the author of my faith. Not only did He plant it in me, He will perfect it. Whew! What a relief! I just need to cooperate with God—not produce faith on my own.

Author and Perfecter

Author and perfecter of my faith: what a wonderful thought!

So often I try to increase my faith, but it all comes to naught.

I was brought up to believe—nurtured from childhood,

But sometimes I question the depth of my faith and get caught up in trying to be good.

When I am worried and troubled, when I feel scared and alone,

I find myself trying hard to muster up faith on my own.

I ask God to forgive me—I should be able to stand,

And God gently reminds me that's not the nature of His plan.

When my faith needs bolstering, it's not up to me;

That's not the way God designed it to be.

So I don't have to come up with faith; God's already planted it within,

I just need to cooperate and let His harvest begin.

I don't have to perfect my faith and make it what it "needs to be."

I just need to yield to God and watch Him work in me.

Thank You, Lord, for choosing me, for making me complete.

Thank You, Lord, for living in me where my weakness and Your grace meet.

Yes, thank You, Lord, for planting seeds of faith in me and for preparing them for harvest. I pray for a bountiful harvest—faith firmly established in You and by You. I'm counting on You, Lord. Amen.

Day 17

"Do not store up for yourselves treasures on earth, where moth and rust destroy, and where thieves break in and steal. But store up for yourselves treasures in heaven, where moth and rust do not destroy, and where thieves do not break in and steal." Matthew 6:19-20

I memorized this passage as a child. I thought I got the point, but in looking back I realize that I interpreted it narrowly. I saw it as pertaining to money and relating to the distant future. Was I too fond of this world's riches? Did I need to give them up? Ouch! And what kind of treasures would I receive in heaven—years from now? Now I have a broader outlook and regard the verses as pertaining to the present, and they challenge and even excite me. When I do something for Christ and His body, I am making a heavenly deposit. That can't be my motive for obeying Christ, but knowing that God is keeping my real treasure safe is a glorious incentive to lay up treasure in heaven!

Treasure

I really like having stuff—more stuff is even better.

God asks me to be a giver, but often I'd rather be a "getter."

What makes earthly things so appealing? Perhaps it's the security they seem to give,

Not worrying about money and necessities seems an easier way to live.

Lord, help me not to store up treasures here where things are so easily destroyed.

Realign my values, please; greed and selfishness are hard to avoid.

I guess it's not always about money, we can treasure other things, too.

If I love anything more than You, God, it's an idol—a hard fact but true.

Sometimes I misplace my treasure by putting things ahead of You—

The opinions of others, leisure, even family, just to name a few.

So how do I go about storing up treasure, not here but in heaven above?

It involves what I value most, it entails service and love.

Money is fine if I don't love it too much, if I don't make it the object of my trust.

I need to remember I won't take it with me, ashes to ashes, dust to dust.

Living well before others is a good thing, I'm called to let my light shine,

Loving and serving family and friends should be a priority of mine.

But my top priority is doing God's will, honoring Him each day as Lord.

Sharing my wealth and serving His world will show where my treasure is stored.

Lord, *You* are my treasure. Don't let me get distracted. May I honor and desire You more than anyone and anything else. Amen.

Day 18

"Give all your worries and cares to God, for he cares about what happens to you." 1 Peter 5:7 (NLT)

This verse does not say, "give *some* of your worries to God"; it does not say, "Give your *big* worries to God"; it says "Give *all* your worries to God." When I have a serious problem, I almost always pray fervently and I trust that He cares. But too often when I have a minor upset, I try to take care of it myself; it may not even occur to me to take it to God. And if it does, I'm reluctant to ask the mighty God of the universe to help me with such a trivial matter. But He assures us that He cares about *all* our concerns—big and small--because He cares about us.

God Cares

Give all your worries and cares to God, for He cares what happens to you.

He offers to carry your burdens, all of them—not just a few.

He doesn't limit His offer—no helping just a bit.

He's willing to take your worry—not some, but all of it.

Sometimes it's hard to release your pain; you want to hold on tight.

It's hard to give up all control and trust God to make things right.

But that's what He wants for His children, it's what He asks you to do.

Give your worries and cares to Him, for He cares what happens to you.

Thank You, Lord, for caring about what happens to me—not just the big stuff but the small stuff, too. Sometimes the trivial day-to-day matters nag at me more than the bigger issues. Nudge me to talk to You throughout the day about *all* my concerns. Amen.

Day 19

"Rejoice in the Lord always. I will say it again: Rejoice!" Philippians 4:4

". . . for the joy of the Lord is your strength." Nehemiah 8:10

Suffering, poverty, and prejudice abound in this world. There's no denying that. Some people seem to think that the sad state of affairs is reason to deny God's existence or at least His love. How sad to assume that God is responsible for the suffering. How sad to assume that He doesn't care and share in our suffering, to forget that He cries with us. How sad to forget that no matter what we suffer here and now, we have an eternity with no suffering in sight if Jesus is our Savior. Now that's cause to rejoice!

Choose Joy

"Rejoice in the Lord always, and again I say, Rejoice!"

Really, Lord? In the midst of all our suffering is gladness even a choice?

With so much sickness and suffering, loss, depression, and grief,

Anger, division, and prejudice, where do we find relief?

Where do we find hope? How do we rejoice?

I guess when it comes down to it, it has to be a choice.

Sometimes what we seek is happiness when things are right and fun,

Joy is found when we comprehend our status in God through His Son.

Regardless of my circumstances I'm destined for a home above!

What greater joy can I feel than to be carried by God's love?

So, yes, I choose to focus on Jesus, and to follow Him day by day.

How do I find gladness and joy? Through Jesus—the Source and the Way!

This is the day You have made, Lord. I will rejoice! I will rejoice that I belong to You and that You're leading me day by day to everlasting joy when I will live with You forever! Amen.

Day 20

"The Lord your God is with you, he is mighty to save. He will take great delight in you, he will quiet you with his love, he will rejoice over you with singing." Zephaniah 3:17

We are told to abide in Christ, to stay with Him. (John 15:5)

We are told to delight in the Lord. (Psalm 37:4)

We are told to love the Lord. (Deuteronomy 6:5)

And we are told to rejoice in the Lord and to sing. (Psalms 68:3 and 66:1)

Zephaniah 3:17 amazes me because it reassures me that God reciprocates! He is with me! He takes delight in me! He loves me! He rejoices over me with singing! How can I not be in awe of the God who is with me, who loves me, who finds me delightful, who rejoices over me, and who sings over me?

God with Me

The Lord is with me—He always has been.

Even when I don't feel it, He's beside me and within.

A dear friend, it's like I'm His favorite one;

Through good times and through bad times, I am never alone!

The Lord is mighty to save, and He saves me,

Not only in this life, but for eternity!

When my path is hard and I don't know what to do

He may not remove the obstacles, but He will lead me through.

The Lord greatly delights in me!

What a miracle of love! How could that be?

He calls me to rejoice and delight in Him, I know,

But that He delights in me seems too good to be so.

He quiets me with His love, then I can hear

When He whispers His assurance that He indeed is near.

This world is loud and busy with demands that never cease,

But if I am quiet before Him, He fills me with His peace.

Can you hear God singing? He's rejoicing over me!

Imagine that—God rejoicing musically!

It makes my heart happy, it is a joyous thing,

That sometimes when God rejoices, He opens His mouth to sing!

I stand in awe of You, God; You minister so tenderly

To all of Your creation—all, and that includes me.

Let me never take for granted Your love and Your care.

May I respond with love and faith, this is my heartfelt prayer.

Thank You, God, for singling me out to love! Thank You for being with me, for saving me—daily, and for comforting me with your love. I am delighted and humbled that You delight in me and rejoice over me! I praise You, Lord! Amen.

Day 21

"After this manner therefore pray ye: Our Father which art in heaven, Hallowed be thy name. Thy kingdom come. Thy will be done in earth, as it is in heaven. Give us this day our daily bread. And forgive us our debts, as we forgive our debtors. And lead us not into temptation, but deliver us from evil: For thine is the kingdom, and the power, and the glory, forever. Amen." Matthew 6:9-13 (KJV)

How many times have I repeated the Lord's Prayer? We say it just about every week in church. I have said it countless times. Yet how many times have I just said it by rote, thinking little about what I'm saying? And when I do think about the words, do I really mean them—those phrases about God's will being done, my forgiving those who have wronged me, staying away from temptation? Do I *say* the Lord's Prayer or do I *pray* the Lord's Prayer?

Reflections on the Lord's Prayer

Sometimes looking at opposites opens up my eyes,

And I see hidden motives and ideas, much to my surprise.

When I pray as Jesus taught, I'm praying in His will,

But only if my heart is honest, and what I say I feel.

When I pray the "Lord's Prayer," am I sincere,

Or if you could know my heart, is this what you would hear?

Our Father which art in heaven,

    Remote and far away;

    Do You even hear me, care what I have to say?

Hallowed be thy name.

    Never a day goes by that You're not defamed.

    Do You really care how we use Your name?

Thy kingdom come,

    Do I mean that when I pray?

    Can that even happen in our world today?

Thy will be done,

    Oops, did I say, "thy"?

    In day-to-day life, far too often I substitute "My."

In earth as it is in heaven.

    I don't get this; I wonder how

Your will could prevail in the here and now.

Give us this day our daily bread.

Just my needs will never do,

If the truth be known, I like my wants, too.

And forgive us our debts

I make "mistakes" time and again,

I wouldn't go so far as to call it sin.

As we forgive our debtors.

Really? Forgive those who hurt me?

Don't I have every right to be angry?

And lead us not into temptation

Don't let me be tempted to sin,

But when the door opens, let me set my toe in.

But deliver us from evil.

Certainly You don't mean a little sin

Can open the door and let the devil in.

For Thine is the kingdom and the power and the glory forever.

Yes, Your kingdom's coming some day

But that seems a long way away.

Jesus, You taught us how to pray,

Help me embrace Your will when I say:

Our Father who art in heaven,

    You're in heaven but also in my heart

    And You're my daddy, and that's the best part.

Hallowed be Thy name.

    Your name is holy—to be revered and adored,

    You are precious Father and Righteous Lord.

Thy kingdom come, Thy will be done

    Thy kingdom come—in my heart,

    Thy will be done—in my heart,

    Right now—each day from the start.

In earth as it is in heaven.

    Lord, help me to submit right now,

Living in Your kingdom—show me how.

Give us this day our daily bread.

Thank You, Lord, that You provide

And that it's daily that our needs are supplied.

And forgive us our debts,

Forgive me for all my sin—

My deeds, my inaction, my thoughts within.

As we forgive our debtors.

With my confession, Your forgiveness is free,

Help me to be as gracious forgiving others as You are to me.

And lead us not into temptation,

Lord, shore me up when I'm tempted to stray,

Lead me out; You've promised to make a way.

But deliver us from evil.

When the devil attacks, help me to resist.

Give me authority to make him cease and desist.

For Thine is the kingdom and the power and the glory forever.

One day every tongue will confess Jesus is Lord, and every knee will bow,

May I worship You, profess You, and serve You right now!

Amen.

So be it!

Thank You, Jesus, for teaching us to pray. Thank You, too, for modeling a life of prayer. Forgive me for taking the privilege of prayer—of talking to my Creator—for granted. May my life be defined by prayer. Amen.

Day 22

"Therefore, there is now no condemnation for those who are in Christ Jesus." Romans 8:1

"No condemnation for those who are in Christ Jesus"—can you take it in? *No* condemnation. I was suffering from a guilty conscience—and I do mean suffering—even though I had confessed my sin. I read this verse and the impact it had on me was freeing. God had forgiven me—completely and absolutely. There was no blame or shame. No "Remember when . . . ? Don't do it again." Just, "You're forgiven and righteous in my sight."

No Condemnation

I know that if we repent and confess

  Jesus is faithful to forgive our sin.

But it's hard to believe it's completely gone

  When I'm still so flawed without and within.

When I confess and God forgives

  Does He really let go and forget?

If He doesn't but holds on instead,

    Then I owe an impossible debt.

But I'm promised no condemnation,

    No more blame—none at all.

When I bring up my sinful past,

    Does Jesus say, "I don't recall"?

It's hard to comprehend the depth of God's love;

    It's easy to question the grace I've received.

But when the enemy condemns and accuses

    Jesus says, "Not guilty! I atoned; she believed."

Thank You, Lord, for this wonderful gift:

    Forgiveness and no condemnation!

Thank You, Lord, for Your wonderful work:

    In You, I am a new creation!

Jesus, I'm amazed by Your grace. Thank You for forgiving *all* my sin. Make me new in You! Amen.

Day 23

"I pray that you will begin to understand the incredible greatness of his power for us who believe him. This is the same mighty power that raised Christ from the dead and seated him in the place of honor at God's right hand in the heavenly realms." Ephesians 1:19-20 (NLT)

This verse astounds me. God's Word says that the same power that He used to raise Jesus from the dead works in me! I don't claim to understand it; perhaps in large part it means that just as Jesus was raised from the dead, so will I be. But I think it must be more: why is it in me now if it's only for when my body dies? Perhaps it refers to the new creation God is making of me. ("Therefore, if anyone is in Christ, he is a new creation; the old has gone, the new has come!" 2 Corinthians 5:17) That transformation is not something I can achieve on my own; it is only through the power of God that this change can occur. Maybe that's how His resurrection power is manifested in me.

Resurrection Power

How can it be, Lord,

That Your power is in me, Lord—

The resurrection power of Jesus!

Help me to believe, Lord,

That it's mine to receive, Lord—

The resurrection power of Jesus!

I feel so weak, Lord,

But this is what You speak, Lord—

The resurrection power of Jesus!

It's impossible for You to lie, Lord,

So help me to rely, Lord,

On the resurrection power of Jesus.

What will this power do, Lord?

This mighty power from You, Lord—

The resurrection power of Jesus?

It will cleanse and save me, Lord.

Bless the life You gave me, Lord,

This resurrection power of Jesus!

It will help me overcome, Lord,

It will lead me to my home, Lord,

This resurrection power of Jesus!

You raised Jesus from the dead, Lord,

Just like You had said, Lord.

That's the resurrection power of Jesus!

So show me how, Lord,

To appropriate Your power, Lord—

The resurrection power of Jesus!

I yield to You, Lord,

Make my heart new, Lord.

In the resurrection power of Jesus!

Lord, help me not to limit Your power in my life but to be open to all that You want to do in me and through me. Help me to take You at Your word and believe that Your mighty power is at work in me. Amen.

Day 24

". . . and let us run with perseverance the race marked out for us."
Hebrews 12:1

Aging is a funny thing. In some ways I still feel young, but I know I'm looking older when strangers say, "Yes Ma'am," and call me Honey. Sometimes some achy bones remind me. It can make me question what's next—does God still have work for me to do? Sometimes I want to take life easy and at other times I want to accomplish new things. The writer of Hebrews compares life to a race, one that should be run with perseverance to the end. I want to run well as long as the Lord leads and enables me, not live like the race ended sometime ago and now it's time to coast—where's the satisfaction in that?

Race? I'm Old!

Life is a race and we're to run it well with faith of mind, soul, and heart.

I look at my placement on the path and I'm nearer the end than the start.

Inside I still feel young, but the numbers say otherwise.

How and when did I get old? How did it catch me by surprise?

Overall, I feel quite well; oh, I have some creaks and aches,

Then there's the memory thing; when did that go, for goodness sakes?

I know that it's a blessing to live long and grow old,

But when the years start adding up, it can be scary if the truth be told.

What's going to happen? How will things go?

Will my health and energy stay strong, or will my mind and my step get slow?

I guess it's that control issue—I want to know what lies ahead;

But God's the One who's in control; He says to let go and trust Him instead.

One concern is my life's purpose; does He still have work for me to do?

And there I go again—that's His call, too.

I know I need to trust in God, He doesn't speak of a retirement plan:

Moses got his call at eighty, and how about Sarah and Abraham?

So, yes, God has a plan for me; that's what He always said,

If there's nothing left in His plan, I wouldn't be here—I'd be dead!

So back to this race we all run—it isn't over yet.

We don't stop before the finish line—there's a prize we want to get.

So I may be older than I feel, but I still have things to do.

Praise God! He still uses me and will till the race is through.

And so for now I'll persevere; there's a race to be run.

And when I cross the finish line, I hope to hear, "Well done!"

Lord, help me to live each day as if it matters because it certainly does! Remind me of that when I get lazy. Help me to run the race well all the way to the finish line! Amen.

Day 25

"For this world is not our home; we are looking forward to our city in heaven, which is yet to come." Hebrews 13:14 (NLT)

Have you ever been homesick? I have. I missed the comfort, the love, the security, the familiarity of home. I suspect that when we get really discouraged with life and its trials, it's a bit of homesickness for heaven. We long for the comfort of our Savior, for the love that abounds there and is not tainted by this world, for the security of dwelling in God's presence, for the familiarity of feeling perfectly comfortable with God and loved ones who are already there. Though it is a little unnerving to think of leaving this world and our loved ones who are still here for now, I suspect that when we arrive in heaven we will be totally at peace and we will know we are where we are meant to be—at home at last.

Missing Home

It brings me joy to travel, to visit places I've never been;

I'm excited to explore new venues, to see things I've never seen.

I love the excitement of vacations, traveling across this land,

I am awed by the beauty I see there and want to see all that I can.

I can't begin to describe the grandeur of mountains and valleys and plains,

The diversity fills my senses and I'm amazed by God again.

Then vacation is over, the time to leave has come;

And, yes, it saddens me to go, but I realize I'm missing my home.

I love short trips, too; I'm blessed to live near the shore,

And though it's quite familiar, there are few places I enjoy going more.

We go there every summer and are joined by family,

Could any reunion be better than togetherness by the sea?

I love to be there with our daughters and with our four grandkids, too.

With the ocean, the sand, the attractions—there are always things to do.

When that blessed gathering is over and the time to leave has come,

I say a sad good-bye to the ocean but I realize I'm missing my home.

It occurs to me—no matter where I go, no matter how much fun it's been,

When the time comes to leave I'm ready for home again.

There's something comforting about home, a peace that in this world is rare,

No matter where I may go, I leave a part of me there.

One day I'll embark on a new journey to a place that's most beautiful of all,

I'll be reunited with my loved ones when God makes His final call.

My heart's not troubled, for Jesus is there, and He's prepared a room for me;

I'm sure it will be to my liking, it's designed for eternity.

And as I drink in heaven's wonders, its beauty beyond compare,

I'm sure I won't be missing my home, I'll know I'm already there.

Thank You, Lord, for the wonderful promise of heaven. As I live day to day, as I live *today*, help me to set my eyes on the prize: eternity spent with You. Amen.

Day 26

"Trust in the Lord with all your heart and lean not on your own understanding; in all your ways acknowledge him, and he will make your paths straight." Proverbs 3:5-6

Sometimes I feel like I am good at trusting God, and sometimes I just can't get over myself! "Lean not on your own understanding." I want to figure things out, to have the answers. That's not the way trust works. If I can remember that God's wisdom is as far above mine as the heavens are above the earth (Isaiah 55:9), maybe I will take to heart how foolish—and how limiting—it is for me to rely on myself and my own understanding. I'm not the one who can make my paths straight; only God can do that.

Trust

"Trust in the Lord with all your heart"

God wants me to trust Him with all my heart,

Not just a little bit, not just a part.

"And lean not on your own understanding,"

I want to figure things out, to determine my own plans,

God wants me to rely on Him, not always have to understand.

"In all your ways acknowledge him"

Life's not compartmentalized—some for Him and some for me,

He wants everything—my life in its entirety.

"And he will make your paths straight."

Sometimes the path seems crooked, God's plans, concealed;

But why would God call me to follow if His guidance isn't revealed?

So God, You seem to say,

That this is the way:

1. Trust You in all I do.

2. Put a check on my own intellect.

3. Every day, live Your way.

Lord, I know You're not a God of 1, 2, 3's—

"If you want this result, follow these."

But You are a God of principles with promises You keep,

And I know that most often what we sow is what we reap.

So help me sow trust, depending on You,

Giving You honor in all that I do.

Design my path before me, make it clear and straight,

Help me walk it faithfully, right up to heaven's gate!

Lord, help me to put my trust in You—completely and wholeheartedly. You alone know what is best for me. Guide me in the paths You have chosen for me. Help me to depend on You more and on myself less. Amen.

Day 27

"Though the fig tree does not bud and there are no grapes on the vines, though the olive crop fails and the fields produce no food, though there are no sheep in the pen and no cattle in the stalls, yet I will rejoice in the Lord, I will be joyful in God my Savior." Habakkuk 3:17-18

There are circumstances in life that I cannot control. I cannot control an unwanted medical diagnosis. I cannot control the economy that decreases my earning power. I cannot even control the driver that rudely cuts me off. But with God's help, I can control my reactions. I can become angry or fearful or bitter: life is often unfair. Or I can choose to embrace life with joy—not because I am denying reality, but because I am looking to ultimate reality—my relationship with Jesus Christ, who is my Rock and my Salvation, my Fortress and my Joy. My joy is in my God—not in my life circumstances.

Joy

When my fig tree buds and there are grapes on my vine,

I'm doing well and I feel just fine.

When my olive crop is good and my fields produce food,

    I'm doing well and everything's good.

When there are plenty of sheep and cows in the stall,

    I'm doing well—no worries at all.

It's easy to feel good when things are fine,

    I feel secure—the world is mine!

It's easy to say, "Praise God, He's good"

    When everything's going just as it should.

But when my vines are empty, my fig tree cursed,

    My crops barren, my fortune reversed,

Then praise comes harder, it sticks in my throat,

    I try to sing but it's just a sour note.

It's not easy to sing my life's song

    When everything around me seems to be wrong.

So, Lord, help me learn what Habakkuk knew—

    That regardless of circumstance I can rejoice in You!

Life is not about riches and things,

God loves the poor man as much as the king.

Joy doesn't come from treasures I've stored,

I'm happy because I belong to the Lord!

May my joy be in You, Lord, and not in temporary things. Remind me that I'm living in Your kingdom now—that Your kingdom has already come in my heart. I am Yours, Lord, and You are mine. That's joy, Lord. Amen.

Day 28

"I have told you these things, so that in me you may have peace. In this world you will have trouble. But take heart! I have overcome the world." John 16:33

When I think about God's promises, I find comfort in His promises of love, forgiveness, salvation. But this verse states a promise that is not among my favorites: in this world we will have trouble. However, there is a sense in which these words of Jesus are reassuring. In the real world we know that we *do* have troubles, so it's reassuring to know that they are to be expected, that they are part of our growth in His Kingdom. It is even more encouraging to be reminded that Jesus also faced troubles and that He overcame the world. Somehow, we share in His victory!

Take Heart

"In this world you will have trouble. But take heart! I have overcome the world."

This verse is encouraging to me,

Though the promise isn't quite what I'd like it to be.

I'd prefer:

"In this world you will have trouble,

Take heart! Problems will burst like a bubble."

I'd like my troubles gone, my problems solved.

I'd like my conflicts quickly resolved.

I'd like Jesus to take my problems away,

But that's not what the words in this verse say.

Yes, sometimes things will get rough,

But Jesus has overcome, and that's enough.

He didn't have it easy, He endured scorn and shame,

But even in death, He overcame.

Jesus, You abide in me and I in You,

So Your victory can be my victory, too.

Forgive me, Lord, for wanting the quick fix—problems over and done,

Help me to trust You completely, to know in You I'll overcome.

And what does that look like? I'm not sure I know,

But God promises to work for my good and I choose to believe that's so.

My problems do not define me, this world is not my home.

I'm wrapped up in Jesus and through Him, I, too, will overcome.

Lord, I don't like trouble; nobody does. But life includes both good times and hard times. Help me to trust You in my troubled times and remember that You experienced greater hardship here than I ever will. You overcame and so will I. My victory is found in You, Lord. Thank You! Amen.

Day 29

"Therefore do not worry about tomorrow, for tomorrow will worry about itself . . ." Matthew 6:34

I know worry is a waste of time, that it accomplishes nothing except making me fret. I know that so often what I worry about never even happens. If it does happen, I suffer twice: once while I worry and then as it happens. So why do I keep worrying? I suspect that worry is a part of our human condition, but if I'm honest, my worry is rooted in a lack of trust. God is sovereign, and He is more than able to take care of me in all situations.

Live in the Present

Lord, teach me to live in the confines of the here and now.

I tend to question the future, I want to control it somehow.

Things may be fine now, but I worry about tomorrow,

Remind me that regardless, You're in my joy and in my sorrow.

I get caught up in my concerns—my frets and my care,

I say that I trust You but act like You're not there.

I fear I'll get ill, injured, whatever—so much to worry about,

Nothing's even wrong now, but I wear myself out.

I worry about my loved ones and the problems that they face,

Help me yield them to You and Your loving embrace.

When they're troubled, I want to fix things, make everything fine,

But You know what's best, so that's Your job, not mine.

Yes, Lord, teach me to live in the present, in the here and now,

To trust that nothing will happen that You don't allow.

And whatever You allow, You'll be present, ever near,

And that can bring me peace of mind and eliminate my fear.

Lord, my mind needs a tune-up. Please tweak my confidence so that I remember that You are in charge. Help me to trust You to take care of me and my loved ones. Help me to live in the present and not in the future of "what-if's." With my mind, I believe Your promise; move that faith into my heart, too. Amen.

Day 30

"... The Lord does not look at the things man looks at. Man looks at the outward appearance, but the Lord looks at the heart." 1 Samuel 16:7

Sometimes I am not totally honest about the "inside" me. I want others to think well of me, and it is embarrassing to bare my soul to others and even to God. I know nothing is hidden from God, but sometimes I still find it difficult to acknowledge my weaknesses—my sins—to God and even to myself. I guess I fear that if I admit them, then I need to start turning from my sin. But when I "come clean" with God and let Him love me and work on me, a weight is lifted and I am freed to be myself.

The Heart of the Matter

What I show you, what I let you see

Isn't always honest, it's not the real me.

There are areas of my life that I choose to hide;

I may not let you see what's really inside.

I don't want you to see the pride and jealousy,

I only want to show you the better, upgraded me.

I'd be embarrassed if you really knew

Some of the things I think, some of the things I do.

But when I choose to live this way, there is a disturbing part,

And that is that God sees straight into my heart.

With Him, there's no deception, no use for a façade

Because absolutely nothing is hidden from our God.

But then again, is that disturbing, something to dread,

Since Jesus looks not with anger, but with love instead?

He doesn't examine to accuse and condemn,

He softens my heart to make me like Him.

So when I'm honest and open with Him

He gently works to deal with my sin.

Relying on Him brings me peace and rest

Since He is the One who loves me best.

Since no one else loves me as much as God,

I can open up to Him with nothing to hide.

So, Jesus, I surrender my heart to You,

May what You see there be what I show others, too.

Thank You, God, for loving me unconditionally—faults and all. Help me to be transparent and to share myself and Your love with others. Amen.

Day 31

"Jesus answered, 'I am the way and the truth and the life . . . '" John 14:6

During a time of earnest prayer one evening, I asked God to help me to know Him better, to understand more fully who He really is. There are four Gospels to tell us about Jesus, but what is the Father really like? Sometimes He seems more mysterious. While I was praying, I felt this verse speaking in my heart. I felt that God was showing me that I can observe the life of Jesus in some detail and that Jesus was sent not only for our salvation but also to show us who God really is. To know the Son is to know the Father.

The Way, the Truth, and the Life

I asked God to reveal Himself: "Let me know You, I pray!"

Jesus nudged me gently and softly whispered, "I Am the Way."

I sought God—to see Him clearly, things get distorted on this earth,

Jesus nudged me gently and softly whispered, "I Am the Truth."

I asked God to help me live well, there's so much confusion and strife,

Jesus nudged me gently and softly whispered, "I Am the Life."

The Way, the Truth, the Life: Jesus is all three;

He shows us the very heart of God: in Jesus, it's God that we see. (John 14:9)

Sometimes the Father seems more aloof, shrouded in mystery;

Jesus clears this up for us: "You've seen God if you've seen me."

I'm beginning to see the message here: To know the Father, look at the Son,

Jesus made it very clear, Son and Father—they are One.

Thank You, Father, for revealing Yourself to us. In Jesus we find our way to You; in Him we find ultimate truth and abundant life; and in Him we understand better Who You are! Amen.

Vignettes

"He will feed his flock like a shepherd. He will carry the lambs in his arms, holding them close to his heart . . ." Isaiah 40:11 (NLT)

With Jesus as my Shepherd,

The very best part

Is that when He carries me

I'm right next to His heart!

"Surely goodness and mercy shall follow me all the days of my life . . ." Psalm 23:6 (KJV)

Whatever my circumstances may be

Your goodness and mercy follow me.

With goodness and mercy You pursue,

Thankfully I can't outrun You.

"... Come before his presence with singing." Psalm 100:2 (KJV)

Do we enter His presence when we sing,

Or when we enter, is a song what we bring?

Is a song the method or the offering?

"Know ye that the Lord, he is God . . ." Psalm 100:3 (KJV)

We are an arrogant lot,

Thinking we're in charge when we're not.

Help me remember You are God alone,

And You—not I—are on the throne.

"And we know that God causes everything to work together for the good of those who love God and are called according to his purpose for them." Romans 8:28 (NLT)

When things don't go as I think they should,

I'll remind myself that God works for my good.

As I love Him and submit to His will,

He'll see that His good plan for me is fulfilled.

(Note to self: Remember, HIS good plan, not mine)

Daily Questions for Reflection

Day 1: Can you recall a time when you felt God's presence in a special way? When were you last still? What prevents you from being still?

Day 2: When have you felt God (or thought perhaps it was God) prompting you to speak to someone or help someone? Will you pray that God will open your eyes to the needs of those you meet today and give you the courage to reach out to them and the words to say?

Day 3: Because morning happens—well, every morning—it's easy to forget that each day is a gift and not just a routine. If you did regard each day as a gift, how might that change your outlook throughout the day?

Day 4: Will you remember to watch and wait for God's blessings and answers to prayer today? Will you seek God's peace and take it to bed with you tonight?

Day 5: What events from the Bible can you remember that give you courage for today? What events from your past remind you that Jesus is faithful and will continue to take care of you?

Day 6: What areas of your faith need shoring up? Will you ask God to help you with your faith?

Day 7: Do you more often follow the flock or the Shepherd? Have you considered how precious it is that Jesus knows your name and that He wants to be familiar enough to you that you recognize His voice?

Day 8: Do you sometimes feel far away from God? How will you remind yourself that it's just a feeling since God has promised His presence? Will you trust that He *is* with you even when you can't feel Him?

Day 9: "Instead of fear I choose love and grace." Do you think acknowledging God's love and grace and saying no to fear is a choice you can make?

Day 10: If you truly trust that God equips you with love, power, and self-control, how will that change your outlook today?

Day 11: What does it mean to you that God is your Daddy and you're His child? How does that impact your relationship?

Day 12: Is it hard for you just to be quiet and be with God? Does your mind wander? (God understands, by the way.) Will you commit to spending quiet time meditating, reading Scripture, listening to praise music, or whatever turns your mind and opens your heart to God?

Day 13: Have you asked God to make your mind obedient to Him, to conform your thoughts to His? Are you aware of any thought patterns that need to change?

Day 14: What does it mean for the peace of God to guard your heart and mind in Christ Jesus? What would that look like in your life?

Day 15: Think about your plans for the day. How can you invest yourself in your daily tasks so that they have eternal significance? Can you help someone today with a smile, encouragement, gratitude or a prayer?

Day 16: What do you think of the idea that it is God who plants His faith within you and that it is He who will continue to develop it if you allow Him? Does that relieve some pressure? Are you ready to cooperate with Him?

Day 17: What heavenly deposits will you make today?

Day 18: What "little" concerns do you have that you need to share with God? Do you believe He cares? Will you seek His help?

Day 19: What is the difference between happiness and joy? How do *you* go about *choosing* joy?

Day 20: Which statement about God do you find most intriguing: that He is with you, that He saves you, that He delights in you, that He calms you with His love, or that He sings over you? Will you contemplate that statement throughout the day? Enjoy God today!

Day 21: Did you find yourself in any of the statements in the first version of the Lord's Prayer? Did you find any personal challenge in the second version?

Day 22: Is there anything in your past or your present that you're ashamed of? Have you told God? Will you believe that God isn't upset with you? And will you thank Him for His love?

Day 23: Do you sometimes feel powerless? Are you open to believing that God's mighty power lives in you? Will you ask God to move that belief from your head to your heart also?

Day 24: Are you up for the race? Are you prepared with prayer and Bible study? Will you run today with purpose and enthusiasm?

Day 25: Is the prospect of Heaven real to you? Most of us don't want to go now, of course, but do you anticipate it with joy and without fear?

Day 26: Will you seek to trust God today? What difference will it make in your life if you try to see God in everything—even the mundane things—you do today?

Day 27: During trying times will you choose to consciously remember what God *has* done for you, what He *is* doing for you, and what He's *going* to do for you?

Day 28: When you face trouble, are you confident that you will overcome? Are you counting on God to see you through?

Day 29: Will you take this challenge: "Today I will think about today and not worry about what's going to happen tomorrow. I trust God to get me through *this day*"?

Day 30: Will you be open and honest with everyone you meet today, including God?

Day 31: What do you see when you look at Jesus?

Printed in the United States
By Bookmasters